Nursery Rhyme Math
Preschool–Kindergarten

About This Book

Mother Goose meets math in this activity-packed resource! Designed to develop math skills in the earliest years, this wonderful resource features 15 activity-based units, each centered around a different popular nursery rhyme. Each four-page unit (see sample below) provides a wealth of developmentally appropriate experiences that challenge your little learners to explore a variety of mathematical skills, such as understanding one-to-one correspondence, counting, estimating, comparing, sequencing, creating patterns, identifying shapes, and more. The pick-and-choose nature of each unit and the easy-to-read skill lines just below each activity title allow you to quickly and easily select the activities that best meet the needs of your students. What better way to create a solid mathematics foundation for your little learners than by building on their natural love of nursery rhymes!

Sample Unit

Featured Rhyme

Skill Line

Variety of Fun Activities

Pattern Page

Student Practice Page

Table of Contents

Skills Grid 3

Three Little Kittens...4

Baa, Baa, Black Sheep...8

Twinkle, Twinkle, Little Star 12

Humpty Dumpty..16

Hey, Diddle, Diddle 20

Little Bo-Peep 24

Mary, Mary, Quite Contrary..28

Jack, Be Nimble...32

This Little Piggy 36

Jack and Jill...40

One, Two, Buckle My Shoe 44

Old Mother Hubbard 48

Hickory, Dickory, Dock...52

Sing a Song of Sixpence 56

A Tisket, a Tasket...60

www.themailbox.com

©2004 The Mailbox®
All rights reserved.
ISBN #1-56234-602-4

Manufactured in the United States
10 9 8 7 6 5 4 3 2 1

Skill	Three Little Kittens	Baa, Baa, Black Sheep	Twinkle, Twinkle, Little Star	Humpty Dumpty	Hey, Diddle, Diddle	Little Bo-Peep	Mary, Mary, Quite Contrary	Jack, Be Nimble	This Little Piggy	Jack and Jill	One, Two, Buckle My Shoe	Old Mother Hubbard	Hickory, Dickory, Dock	Sing a Song of Sixpence	A Tisket, a Tasket
Number and Operations															
Counting to three	•	•													
Counting to five			•												
Counting to ten					•										
Counting to 24														•	
Understanding one-to-one correspondence	•				•			•							
Counting in sequence						•									
Recognizing numerals													•		
Recognizing and naming written numerals											•				
Understanding the concept of zero												•			
Writing numerals to 12													•		
Comparing a number of sets		•													
Comparing two sets														•	
Identifying ordinal numbers				•											
Sequencing ordinal numbers						•					•				
Combining concrete objects		•													
Separating concrete objects		•													
Adding with concrete objects						•					•	•		•	•
Subtracting with concrete objects						•					•	•			•
Using strategies to solve number problems												•			
Geometry															
Recognizing differences in shapes			•												
Identifying shapes			•				•						•		
Describing shapes			•												
Using positional words	•				•			•	•	•					
Measurement															
Using nonstandard units appropriately				•											
Measuring length with nonstandard units				•	•		•								
Sequencing objects by height							•								
Telling time to the hour													•		
Recognizing coin value (penny, nickel, and dime)														•	
Comparing values of the penny, nickel, and dime									•						
Exploring tools for measuring capacity												•			•
Comparing capacity												•			•
Estimating capacity															•
Data Analysis															
Collecting and displaying data						•			•						•
Algebra															
Creating and extending movement patterns			•												
Creating and extending sound patterns			•												
Creating patterns					•										
Extending patterns					•		•								
Sorting by color	•						•								
Sorting by size				•											
Sorting by type											•				
Sorting and classifying objects								•							•

Three Little Kittens

You can count on these activities to be "purr-fect" for your little kittens!

Three little kittens lost their mittens,
And they began to cry,
"Oh, Mother Dear, we sadly fear
Our mittens we have lost!"
"What? Lost your mittens?
You naughty kittens!
Then you shall have no pie."
"Meow, meow, meow!"

Mitten Match
Number and Operations

• understanding one-to-one correspondence

Cheerful meows will resound as your little kittens successfully pair colorful mittens! To prepare, make a clothesline by securely tying a length of cotton cord between two sturdy chairs as shown. Next, make several colorful construction paper copies of the mitten patterns on page 6. Cut out the mittens and then glue a wooden clothespin to one mitten in each pair. Clip the prepared mittens on the clothesline and store the other mittens in a basket.

Invite one child at a time to choose a mitten from the basket and then match it with one mitten on the clothesline. Have him clip the mitten on the clothesline to make a pair. After he has paired all the mittens, have him count the number of pairs.

To keep student interest high, change the center slightly each day. Add a pair of mittens to the mix (did the kittens make a new friend?) or remove one mitten from the basket (oops! a kitten must have lost a mitten). Meow, meow!

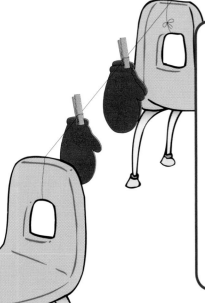

Counting Kittens
Number and Operations

• counting to three

Reinforce counting skills as youngsters help the mama cat find her three little kittens! Have youngsters sit in a circle and ask them to pretend that you are the mama cat and you're looking for your three little kittens. Invite each child to imagine she is a kitten. Choose one, two, or three little kittens to stand; then have the group count the set. Ask youngsters to decide if this set is the mama's little kittens and explain why or why not. Repeat the counting process with different sets of kittens until sets of three have been identified several times. Then, acting as the mama cat, guide all your little kittens to recite and perform the rhyme.

For further counting practice, have each child complete the activity on a copy of page 7. Read the directions to students and then have them color the correct number of kittens in each box.

Missing Mittens!
Geometry

• using positional words

Strengthen your little kittens' understanding of positional words when they help find the lost mittens! Use the patterns on page 6 to prepare three different-colored construction paper mitten cutouts. Then, while students are out of the classroom, hide the mittens in three different positions in a designated area of your classroom. (For example, hide mittens on a rug, under a chair, and beside a bookcase.)

During group time, recite the traditional nursery rhyme with youngsters. Then ask one student to search for a lost mitten. When the child finds a mitten, encourage him to use a positional-word phrase to tell where he found it. Repeat with the remaining two mittens. Next, invite three different students to hide one mitten each in a different position around the classroom. Choose another student to search for a lost mitten and describe its position. Continue the process until each child has had a turn hiding or finding a mitten. What good little kittens!

It's **under** the chair!

Plump Pies
Algebra

• sorting by color

This imaginative sorting center offers youngsters a no-mess way to prepare the perfect pie! In advance, gather a supply of red, blue, and black pom-poms, a large plastic bowl, a large plastic spoon, paper plates, and three aluminum pie pans. Put all the pom-poms in the bowl and mix them together. Then place all the supplies at a center. Encourage youngsters to pretend that the pom-poms are different types of berries that the mama cat uses to make pies for the three little kittens. Invite each child in a small group to scoop a spoonful of berries onto a paper plate. Ask each child to sort the berries by color into different pie pans as shown. The mama cat would be proud of those pies!

5

Mitten Patterns
Use with "Mitten Match" on page 4 and "Missing Mittens!" on page 5.

Name _____

Counting Kittens

Count. 5 4 3 2 1

Color.

1	
3	**2**

©The Mailbox® • *Nursery Rhyme Math* • TEC60814

Note to the teacher: Use with "Counting Kittens" on page 4.

Baa, Baa, Black Sheep

Math enjoyment is in the bag with this collection of learning opportunities designed with your flock in mind!

"Baa, baa, black sheep, have you any wool?"
"Yes, sir! Yes, sir! Three bags full—
One for the master, one for the dame,
One for the little boy who lives down the lane."

Bags of Wool
Number and Operations

• counting to three

How many bags of wool does each sheep need in this center activity? Why, three bags full, of course! Label each of 15 lunch-size paper bags with the word *wool.* Place a small block in each bag for weight. Then stuff each one with newspaper and staple it closed. Make five copies of the sheep pattern on page 10. Cut out each pattern. Then use clear Con-Tact paper to adhere each cutout to the floor in a traffic-free area of the classroom. Place the bags of wool in a large container nearby. A visiting youngster counts orally as he places three bags on each sheep. Then he places the bags back in the container for the next youngster. For additional practice counting to three, have each student complete a copy of page 11.

Scoop and Count
Number and Operations

• comparing a number of sets

Fluffy cotton balls represent wool at this scoop-and-count comparison center! Place the following items at a center: a container of cotton balls, a half-cup measuring cup, and two lunch-size paper bags. A pair of youngsters visits the center. Each child takes a scoop of cotton balls and places it in a bag. Then he dumps out his bag and counts the cotton balls. The children compare the sets and decide who has more wool and who has less, or whether they both have the same (encourage students to line up their cotton balls in one-to-one correspondence). Have the students place their cotton balls back in the container. Then invite them to take another scoop!

Let's Do Lunch!
Number and Operations

• combining concrete objects

What do you get when you combine preaddition skills with hungry sheep? This playful "baa-llad" and activity! Reduce and make ten copies of the sheep pattern on page 10. Then prepare the sheep and four brown construction paper strips for flannelboard use. Place the strips on your flannelboard to resemble a fenced-in pasture. Gather your students in front of the flannelboard. Then place several sheep in the pasture. Sing the song provided with your class, adding more sheep when indicated. Then count the sheep inside the fence with your youngsters. Sing the song several times, combining sheep to create a different total each time.

(sung to the tune of "If You're Happy and You Know It")

Oh, a little flock of sheep is having lunch. (Munch! Munch!)
They are chewing with a loud and noisy crunch! (Crunch! Crunch!)
When you open up the gate,
In come more—they're running late!
Now how many sheep are eating in this bunch? (Munch! Munch!)

Shearing the Sheep!
Number and Operations

• separating concrete objects

Wool gathering is not only encouraged in this small-group game—it's the goal! Make a copy of page 10. Draw ten distinct curlicues on the sheep and then make three copies of it. Color and laminate the sheep if desired. Place the copies at a table along with a container of cotton balls (wool), three lunch-size paper bags, and a simple game spinner labeled with numerals from 1 to 4. (A simple spinner can be made with a tagboard circle, a dull pencil, and an oversized paper clip as shown.) Invite three students to the table. Give each child a sheep and have him place a cotton ball on each curlicue. Also give him a paper bag. A student spins the spinner, removes the corresponding number of cotton balls from his sheep, and then places them in his bag. Encourage each child to count the remaining cotton balls. Have youngsters take turns repeating the process until all of the wool is "sheared" and there are three bags full!

Sheep Pattern
Use with "Bags of Wool" on page 8 and "Let's Do Lunch!" and "Shearing the Sheep!" on page 9.

Name _____

Pull the Wool

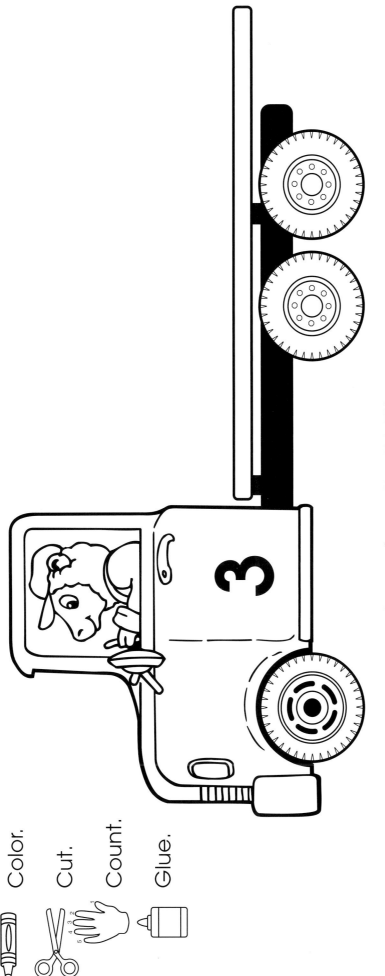

Color.

Cut.

Count.

Glue.

©The Mailbox® • *Nursery Rhyme Math* • TEC60814

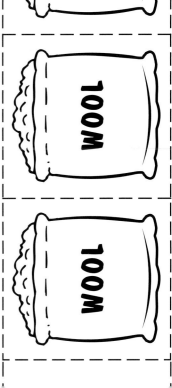

WOOL

WOOL

WOOL

Note to the teacher: Use with "Bags of Wool" on page 8.

11

Twinkle, Twinkle, Little Star

Put a sparkle in youngsters' eyes with this constellation of activities!

> Twinkle, twinkle, little star,
> How I wonder what you are,
> Up above the world so high,
> Like a diamond in the sky.

Five Shining Stars
Number and Operations

• counting to five

One star twinkles and five stars fill the sky in this adorable minibooklet, which reinforces counting skills! To prepare, make a class supply of page 14 and gather 15 star stickers per child. Have each child cut out her cover and pages and then stack them in order. Help her staple the minibooklet along the left side. Next, have her write her name on the cover and read page one. Direct her to color a night sky and then attach the corresponding number of star stickers. Help her continue to read and illustrate each page in this manner. When the minibooklet is complete, invite each child to read it to a partner and then take it home for counting practice with her family. Twinkle, twinkle!

Gather Round!
Geometry

• recognizing differences in shapes

Gather round for a shape awareness activity that everyone can enjoy! In advance, prepare a star wand by taping a craft foam star cutout to a ruler. During circle time, lead students in reciting the rhyme; then show students the star wand and guide them to conclude that the shape is indeed a star. Next, use the wand to point to an example of a circle in your classroom. Have youngsters confirm the shape and tell whether it is the same as or different than the star. Then invite student volunteers to use the wand to point out other examples of circles in the environment, such as a clock. When youngsters have identified several circles, use the star wand to point out another simple shape and repeat the activity in this same manner. Follow up this shape awareness activity by helping each child complete a copy of page 15.

This clock is a circle!

Twinkly Shapes
Geometry

• identifying and describing shapes

Here's a circle. It's round, so it doesn't have any corners.

If you're ready to reinforce shapes, then this is the small-group activity for you! To prepare, cut a variety of stars, circles, squares, rectangles, and triangles from metallic paper and then laminate the shapes if desired. Write the first two lines of the rhyme on a chart and program a different card for each shape's name. With a small group, spread the shapes on a tabletop and then read the rhyme. Encourage a volunteer to look through the shapes and choose a star. Have him describe a star's attributes. Next, attach a prepared card to the chart as shown. Read the rhyme again, substituting the appropriate shape name.

Twinkle, twinkle, little ｜ circle ｜
How I wonder what you are.

Invite a student to pick up the matching shape and describe its attributes. Continue the activity in this manner until each shape has been identified and described. Twinkle, twinkle, little circle!

Is That a Pattern I Hear?
Algebra

• creating and extending patterns with sounds and movements

Diamond, sky, diamond, sky—youngsters will enjoy making patterns they can see *and* hear! To begin, choose a couple of rhyme-related pattern builders (see the suggestions below). Next, gather a small group of students and model a simple AB pattern. Pause and ask a volunteer to join you in duplicating it. Then invite a pair of students to take over and extend the pattern. Create a new pattern with different builders and continue in this manner. For even more pattern reinforcement, encourage each child, in turn, to create a pattern for a partner to duplicate and extend. The sky's the limit!

Pattern Builders		
	Sounds	**Movements**
Twinkle	shake sleigh bells	
Diamond	strike a triangle	
Star	strike a cowbell	
Sky	shake a tambourine	
World	beat a drum	
Little	squeeze a squeaky toy	

Minibooklet Cover and Pages

Use with "Five Shining Stars" on page 12.

Counting Stars

by _____

One star twinkles.   1

Two stars shine.   2

Three stars glow.   3

Four stars sparkle.   4

Five stars fill the sky!   5

14

Name _____

Shapes I See

Color by the code:

◯ red ▭ blue △ green ▢ orange ☆ yellow

Draw a circle.

Draw a square.

Note to the teacher: Use with "Gather Round!" on page 12.

15

Humpty Dumpty

Your little ones are certain to fall for this collection of activities about everyone's favorite egghead!

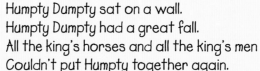

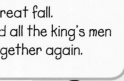

Humpty Dumpty sat on a wall.
Humpty Dumpty had a great fall.
All the king's horses and all the king's men
Couldn't put Humpty together again.

Grade A Sorting
Algebra

• sorting by size

Eggs come in different sizes, and so does Humpty Dumpty in this small-group sorting activity! Make copies of the face patterns on page 18 in three different sizes. Color the patterns and cut them out. Laminate the cutouts for durability and then ready them for flannelboard use. Also cut three egg shapes from white felt, each one sized to match a set of facial features. Next, gather up to three students around your flannelboard. Place the eggs on the flannelboard along with the three eye cutouts. Have each student match a pair of eyes to an egg by size. Continue with each facial feature until each Humpty Dumpty has eyes, a nose, and a mouth in the appropriate size. These eggs are all put together!

Helping Humpty!
Measurement

• using nonstandard units appropriately

These student-made ladders enhance measurement skills and give Humpty Dumpty a helping hand off that wall! Gather a small group of students. Have each youngster color and cut out a copy of the Humpty Dumpty pattern on page 19 and then glue it to the top of a 12" x 18" sheet of red construction paper. Explain that Humpty Dumpty doesn't want to fall, so he needs a ladder to get down safely. Have each child glue two 18-inch brown construction paper strips to the wall to resemble the sides of a ladder. Then invite her to glue short brown construction paper strips between the sides to resemble rungs.

Next, help each child line up building blocks against the edge of the ladder to measure its length. Have each child count the total number of blocks. Then write the number in the space provided on a copy of the poem on page 19. Encourage each youngster to glue the poem next to her ladder. Humpty Dumpty is sure to get down safe and sound!

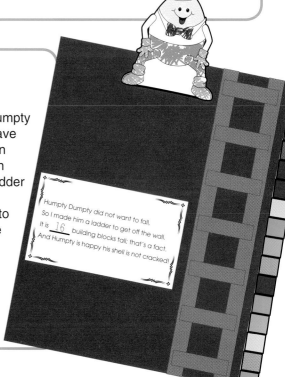

Humpty Dumpty did not want to fall.
So I made him a ladder to get off the wall.
It is __16__ building blocks tall; that's a fact.
And Humpty is happy his shell is not cracked!

How Tall Is the Wall?
Measurement

• measuring length with nonstandard units

With new materials each day, youngsters will never have a dull moment measuring Humpty Dumpty's wall at this center! Draw a brick pattern on three 12" x 18" sheets of red construction paper. Tape the sheets together to make an 18" x 36" length that resembles a wall; then tape it to a tabletop. Next, tape a copy of the Humpty Dumpty pattern on page 19 to the top of the wall as shown. Place a container of craft sticks at the table. A visiting child measures the wall by lining up the craft sticks against the outer edge. Then she counts the number of craft sticks used. Each day replace the measurement materials (see suggestions provided). Let the measuring begin!

Suggested Measurement Materials
blocks
unsharpened pencils
egg cutouts
plastic spoons
drinking straws
crayons
kitchen sponges

Riding to the Rescue!
Number and Operations

• identifying ordinal numbers

All the king's horses and all the king's men help little ones understand ordinal numbers! Make five copies of the horseman pattern on page 18. Color and cut out the patterns. Gather a small group of students at a table. Then place the cutouts in a row on the table. Explain that all the king's horses and all the king's men are riding to go help Humpty Dumpty after his fall. Then ask the students which rider will get there first? Encourage a student to point to the appropriate rider. Then continue asking similar position questions with the ordinal numbers second, third, fourth, and fifth. Once children gain understanding of the activity, challenge them by asking questions out of order or by adding more riders to the row.

Face Patterns
Use with "Grade A Sorting" on page 16.

Horseman Pattern
Use with "Riding to the Rescue!" on page 17.

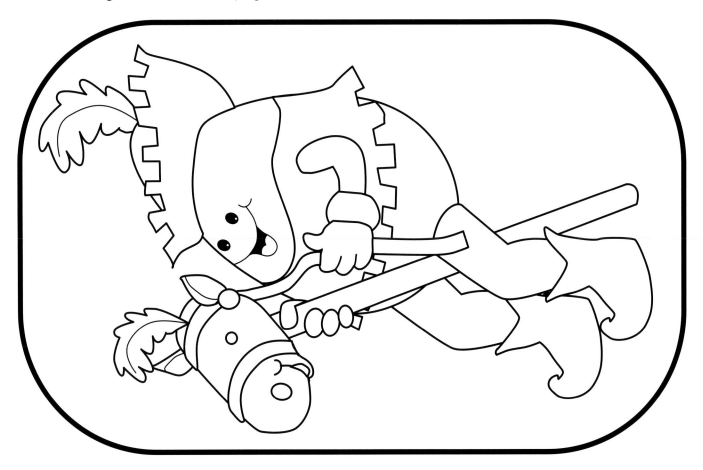

18

Humpty Dumpty Pattern
Use with "Helping Humpty!" on page 16 and "How Tall Is the Wall?" on page 17.

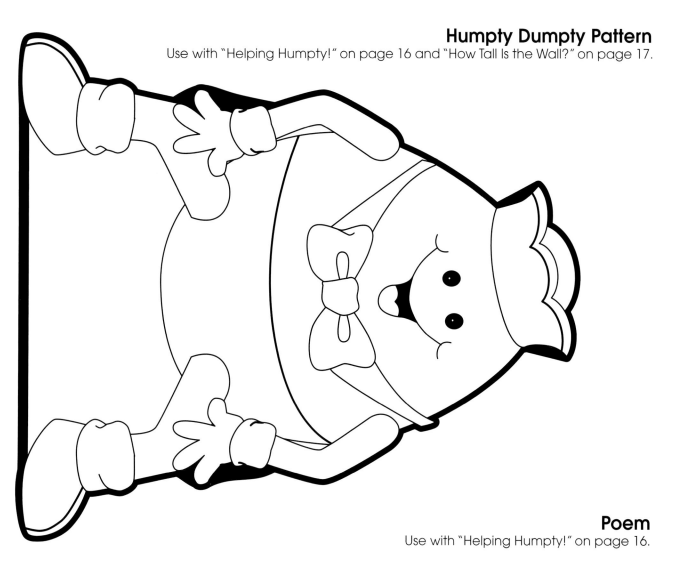

Poem
Use with "Helping Humpty!" on page 16.

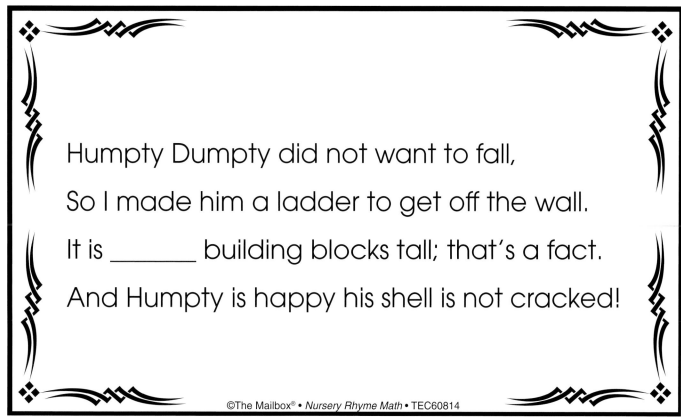

Humpty Dumpty did not want to fall,

So I made him a ladder to get off the wall.

It is _____ building blocks tall; that's a fact.

And Humpty is happy his shell is not cracked!

Hey, Diddle, Diddle
Math is more fun with this entertaining cast of characters!

Hey, diddle, diddle,
The cat and the fiddle,
The cow jumped over the moon;
The little dog laughed
To see such sport,
And the dish ran away with the spoon.

Set the Table
Number and Operations

• counting to ten

• understanding one-to-one correspondence

Dishes and spoons can't really run away, but they can provide plenty of counting practice! Fill a plastic tub with ten paper plates (dishes) and ten plastic spoons. Place the tub in a center with a long table. Invite students at this center to empty the tub and count each set of objects. Next, invite students to pretend to set the table using one-to-one correspondence to match a spoon with each dish. Have students count to check that there are ten sets of spoons and dishes. All set?

China Patterns
Algebra

• creating and extending patterns

Bet your youngsters have never seen china patterns like these before! In advance, make three copies of page 23. If desired, color and laminate the sheets. Then cut apart the pattern cards, place them in a large string-tie envelope, and store the envelope in a center. Invite a pair of students in this center to play this patterning game. One child uses the cards to make a row and shows it to his partner. If she decides the row is a pattern, she extends it. If it is not a pattern, she makes a new row of cards for her partner to examine. Students continue switching roles in this manner to create and extend patterns until the supply of cards is used.

That's a great pattern!

The cow sat UNDER the moon!

The Cow Jumped Under the Moon?
Geometry

• using positional words

Encourage the cow to do more than jump over the moon with this role-playing activity. Duplicate page 22 onto white construction paper to make a class supply. Have each child color and cut out her cow and moon. Help her glue the cow to a sentence strip sized to fit around her head. Next, instruct her to tape the moon cutout to a jumbo craft stick. Review positional words with your group, and then pair students for some active practice. Direct one child in each pair to don her headband, pretend to be the cow, and follow positional directions from her partner. Invite the other child in each pair to hold his moon and give the cow simple directions such as "Stand beside the moon" and "Sit under the moon." After a designated amount of time, have partners switch roles and continue the activity. Then send the headbands and moons home for additional practice.

Wow! My jump is seven shoes long!

START

FINISH

Moon Jump!
Measurement

• measuring length with nonstandard units

Here's a display that will inspire youngsters to try to jump over the moon! In advance, tape a four-foot length of blue bulletin board paper to your floor. Attach a large moon cutout in the middle of the paper and draw a starting line at one end. Have students line up behind the starting line. Tell them that the cow jumped over the moon, and they're going to see how far they can jump. Ask each child, in turn, to stand on the floor beside the starting line and jump as far as he can beside the paper. Use a marker to write his name on the paper, indicating his jump length. After everyone has jumped, enlist student help to measure each length with a child's shoe and write the result beside the appropriate name. Whose jump was closest to the moon? Did anyone jump over it? Discuss the results as a group; then mount the finished display as a lasting reminder of the day students tried to jump over the moon!

Cow and Moon Patterns
Use with "The Cow Jumped Under the Moon?" on page 21.

cow

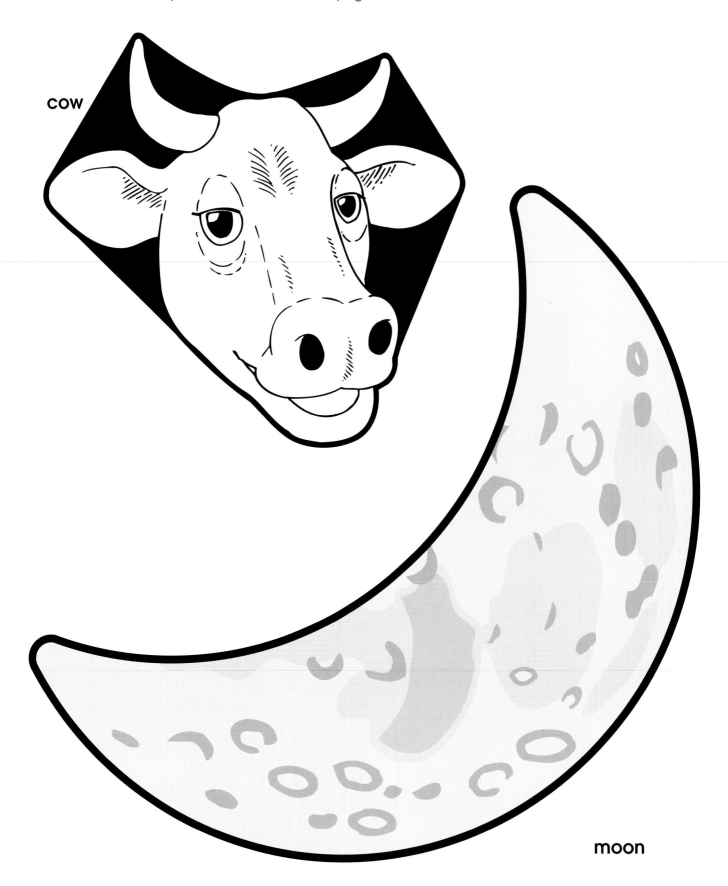

moon

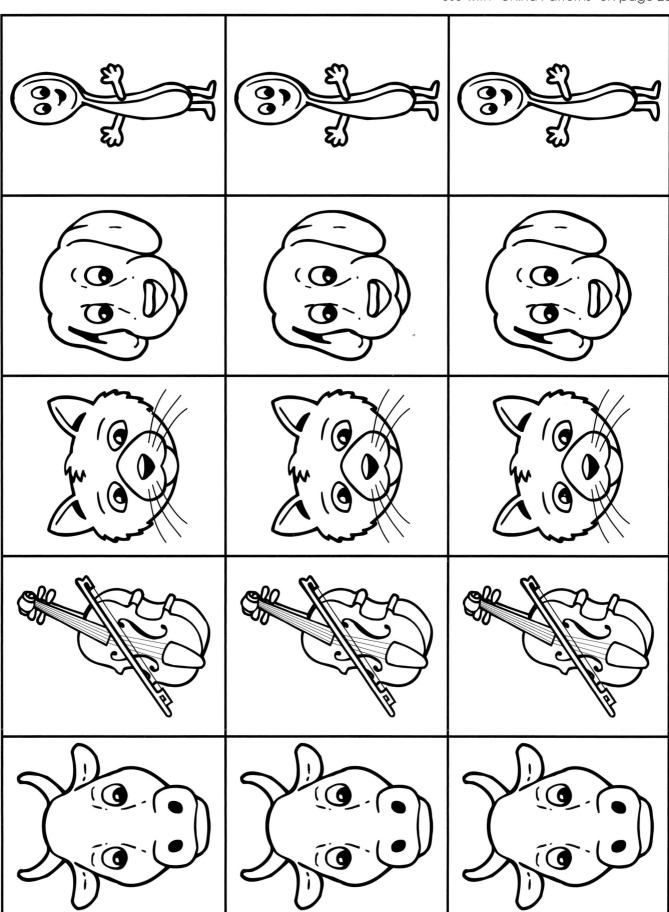

Little Bo-Peep

Your little shepherds will be delighted to tend this flock of activities!

> Little Bo-Peep has lost her sheep,
> And doesn't know where to find them.
> Leave them alone, and they will come home,
> Wagging their tails behind them.

Where Is One Sheep?
Number and Operations

• counting in sequence

This woolly adaptation of a popular call-and-response song makes counting fun for your whole flock! After familiarizing your youngsters with the nursery rhyme, teach them the words and actions to the song below. Then sing the first part of each verse and encourage youngsters to respond while you count to five together.

(sung to the tune of "Where Is Thumbkin?")

Where is [one] sheep? (Where is [one] sheep?)	*Hand behind back.*
Here I am! (Here I am!)	*Bring out one finger.*
Have you seen Miss Bo-Peep? (I have not *seen* Bo-Peep).	*Make fingers "talk" to each other.*
We are lost! (We are lost!)	*Put hand behind back.*

Repeat the verse, substituting two *through* five *where indicated and adding the appropriate number of fingers each time.*

Line Up, Sheep!
Number and Operations

• sequencing ordinal numbers

Little Bo-Peep has found her sheep, and she's ready to try a new plan. She's hoping that keeping the sheep in line will help them stay together. To prepare for this ordinal number activity, duplicate page 26 to make ten sheep. Color and cut out the sheep; then prepare them for flannelboard use. Gather a small group of students and invite them to line up the sheep on a flannelboard and then count them for Little Bo-Peep. Using ordinal words and phrases, ask volunteers to find specific sheep. Which sheep is first? Which sheep is fourth? Where is the second sheep? Conclude the activity by encouraging students to count the total number of sheep again. They're all still there; Little Bo-Peep would be proud!

A Fine Flock
Number and Operations

• adding and subtracting with concrete objects

Poor Bo-Peep! As soon as she finds some of her missing sheep, others run and hide. Invite your youngsters to help Bo-Peep keep her sheep by giving each child in a small group a sheet of green construction paper (pasture) and five cotton balls (sheep). Have each child put one sheep in the pasture. Then have him add two more sheep. Ask a volunteer to count his sheep aloud. Have the rest of the children confirm that there are three sheep in their pastures. Then tell your group that one sheep runs away and each child should subtract one sheep from his pasture. Ask a volunteer how many sheep are left; then have the group count and confirm.

Continue adding and subtracting sheep in this manner until students have practiced adding and subtracting to five. Then help each child complete a copy of page 27 for additional practice.

There are three sheep in the pasture!

Name **Alexander**
Hide-and-Seek Sheep
Add.
Color by the code.

Color Code
2—yellow   3—brown
4—green   5—blue

1 + 1 = **2**
1 + 3 = **4**   5 + 0 = **5**
3 + 2 = **5**
1 + 2 = **3**   2 + 3 = **5**
1 + 4 = **5**
2 + 2 = **4**   4 + 0 = **4**

Look Again
Data Analysis

• collecting and displaying data

Leaving the sheep alone in hopes that they'll return home isn't working very well. Enlist the help of your little ones to bring each sheep safely home! In advance, copy page 26 to make a class supply of sheep; then cut them out. Also make a large three-column graph from bulletin board paper as shown. Title the graph "We Found Little Bo-Peep's Sheep!" and place it in your circle area. While children are out of the room, hide each sheep within easy student reach. When students return, tell them Little Bo-Peep was just there searching for her lost sheep but didn't find any. Ask each child to find one missing sheep. When all the sheep are found, encourage students to compare the sheep and notice the differences. Place the graph on the floor and invite each child with a seated sheep to tape it to the graph in the first column. Repeat with each remaining group of sheep, placing each type of sheep in a different column. Then count and discuss the results. Were there more standing sheep or jumping sheep? How many sheep were found in all? Wow—that's a big flock!

We found Bo-Peep's sheep!

sitting	dancing	standing

Sheep Patterns

Use with "Line Up, Sheep!" on page 24 and "Look Again" on page 25.

Name _____

Hide-and-Seek Sheep

Add.
Color by the code.

Color Code
2—yellow   3—brown
4—green   5—blue

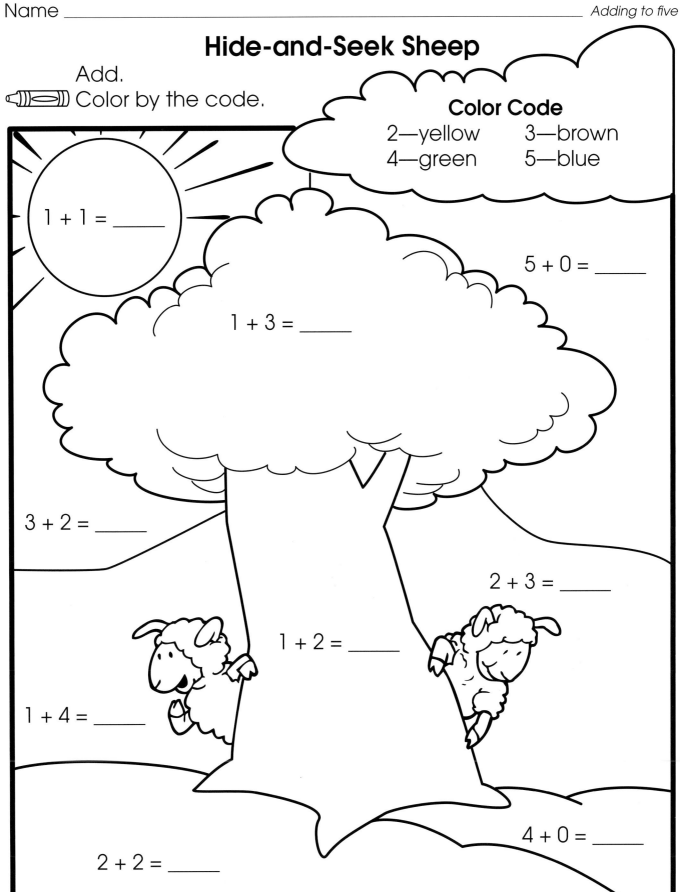

$1 + 1 =$ _____

$5 + 0 =$ _____

$1 + 3 =$ _____

$3 + 2 =$ _____

$2 + 3 =$ _____

$1 + 2 =$ _____

$1 + 4 =$ _____

$4 + 0 =$ _____

$2 + 2 =$ _____

©The Mailbox® • *Nursery Rhyme Math* • TEC60814

Note to the teacher: Use with "A Fine Flock" on page 25.

Mary, Mary, Quite Contrary

Cultivate youngsters' math skills with this colorful bouquet of learning opportunities!

Mary, Mary, quite contrary,
How does your garden grow?
With silver bells and cockleshells
And pretty maids all in a row.

A Shape Garden
Geometry

• identifying shapes

Little ones replace Mary's unusual garden with an equally inventive one full of basic shapes! Cut a circle, square, rectangle, and triangle from household sponges. Then hot-glue an empty film canister to each one to create a handle. Place the prepared sponges in your painting area along with shallow containers of colorful tempera paint and a supply of seven-inch green construction paper strips. Invite one or more students to the area. Each child glues four strips (stems) to a 12" x 18" sheet of white construction paper. Then he uses the prepared sponges to print a different colorful shape (flower) above each stem as shown. Finally, he identifies each flower's shape. When the paint is dry, encourage each student to cut out construction paper leaves and glue them to the stems. Display the shape gardens on a bulletin board with the adjusted nursery rhyme provided. What lovely flowers!

Mary, Mary, quite contrary,
How does your garden grow?
With circles and rectangles, squares and triangles
All lined up in a row.

Planting a Rainbow!
Algebra

• sorting by color

Youngsters make a colorful tabletop garden at this sorting center. No dirt required! Collect pictures of flowers from seed catalogs and magazines (make sure each picture shows a single flower color). Glue each picture to a same-size piece of tagboard and laminate each one. Put the pictures in a container and place it on a table. Tape sheets of construction paper representing each flower color to the tabletop. Then label each sheet with the appropriate color name. A visiting youngster removes each picture and sorts it onto the paper with the matching color. This center brightens everyone's day!

Gardening With Mary
Algebra

• duplicating and extending movement patterns

Even Mary wouldn't be contrary with this action-filled patterning practice! Make four copies of the cards on page 30. Cut out the cards and prepare each one for flannelboard use. Gather students in your large-group area. Then place cards on your flannelboard in an AB pattern. Read the pattern to your class, pantomiming each action shown. Then encourage students to join you in acting out and extending the pattern. When students gain experience with the activity, challenge them by creating more complex patterns, or invite a student to make a pattern on the flannelboard for her classmates to follow!

From Short to Tall
Measurement

• sequencing objects by height

Floral foam and plastic flowers are the fun props needed for this sequencing activity! Trim the stems of four plastic flowers so that each one is a different height. (For safety, place tape around the bottom of each one.) Present the flowers to your youngsters and explain that Mary wants to water the flowers in order from shortest to tallest. Have the students help you place the flowers in the foam in the correct sequence (make sure to push the stems to the bottom of the foam so the height difference can be seen). Then place the foam and flowers at a center for individual student use. For further practice, have each youngster complete a copy of page 31. Sequencing skills are sure to blossom!

Dig.

Sprinkle.

Drop.

Pat.

Name _____

Pots of Posies!

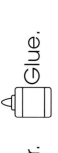 Color.   ✂ Cut out.   Put the flowers in order.   ◁🗔 Glue.

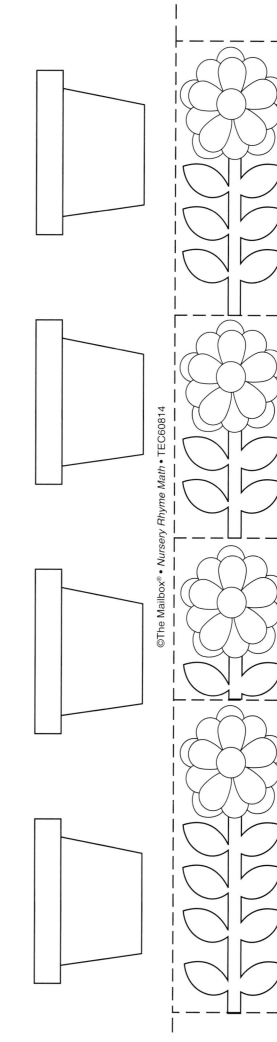

©The Mailbox® • Nursery Rhyme Math • TEC60814

Note to the teacher: Use with "From Short to Tall" on page 29.

Jack, Be Nimble

Little ones will *jump* at the chance to complete these activities!

Jack, be nimble;
Jack, be quick!
Jack, *jump* over the candlestick!

Positions by the Book!
Geometry

• using positional words

Youngsters are in control of Jack's actions in this clever booklet! In advance, make a copy of page 35 for each child. Also make a class supply of the Jack pattern on page 34. Cut a class supply of 4" x 5" construction paper covers. Cut a 12-inch length of yarn for each child.

To begin, give each student a Jack pattern and have her color it as desired. Laminate the patterns and then have each child cut out her pattern. Hole-punch each pattern and tie one end of a yarn length to the hole. Next, give a copy of page 35 to each child. Instruct her to cut out the pages. Help each student stack her pages and then staple them between covers. Hole-punch the corner of each booklet. Next, tie the opposite end of her yarn length to her booklet as shown. Instruct her to trace the dotted words and color the picture on each page. Discuss the similarities and differences of the positional words in the booklet. Then have each child appropriately manipulate Jack as she reads each page. Jack, get moving!

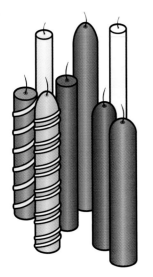

Savvy Candle Sorting
Algebra

• sorting and classifying objects

Brighten students' interest in attributes with this activity! In advance, ask for donations of used and unused candles of various shapes, colors, and sizes. Place the candles on a table and invite a small group of children to join you. Invite each student to examine the candles. Then discuss the candles' similarities and differences. Next, select two attributes, such as tall and short, and have students sort the candles into two groups. After several rounds of sorting using different attributes, sort the candles yourself without identifying the distinguishing attribute(s) you used. Challenge youngsters to determine the sorting attribute(s) by observing the sets of candles.

Candles Measure Up
Measurement

• measuring length with nonstandard units

Jump into this idea, which has youngsters measuring with birthday candles. To prepare, make a copy of the recording sheet on page 34 for each child. Give each student a sheet and a supply of birthday candles. Instruct him to find each object depicted on his paper and then use candles laid end to end to measure it. Instruct him to count the candles and then record the number on his paper. After each child has completed his recording sheet, compare the measurements. There could be more than one correct answer for each measurement, depending on the sizes of various tables, pencils, and books in your classroom!

Going the Distance
Geometry

• using positional words

After reciting the rhyme, spark students' enthusiasm for practicing positional words with this fun activity! Make a class set of the Jack patterns on page 34 and one copy of the candlestick pattern on the same page. Cut headbands from bulletin board paper to make a class set plus one. Have each child color and cut out a Jack pattern and then glue it to a headband. Size each child's headband and staple it. Make a candlestick headband in the same manner. Have students stand in a circle. Choose one child to wear the candlestick headband and stand in the center. Discuss the positional words *near, far,* and *around.* Then have students stand in a circle and hold hands. Instruct the group to move near the candle, move far from the candle, and move around the candle. Repeat the activity until each child has had the chance to glow in the center of the circle!

33

Jack and Candlestick Patterns

Use with "Positions by the Book!" on page 32 and
"Going the Distance" on page 33.

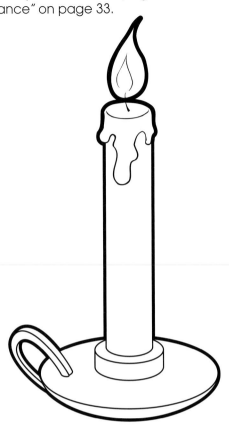

Name _____   Measurement recording sheet

Candle Measurement

Measure.
Record.

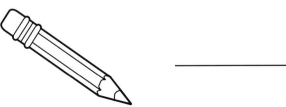 _____

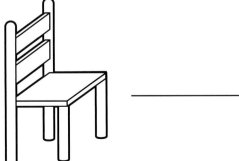 _____

 _____

 _____

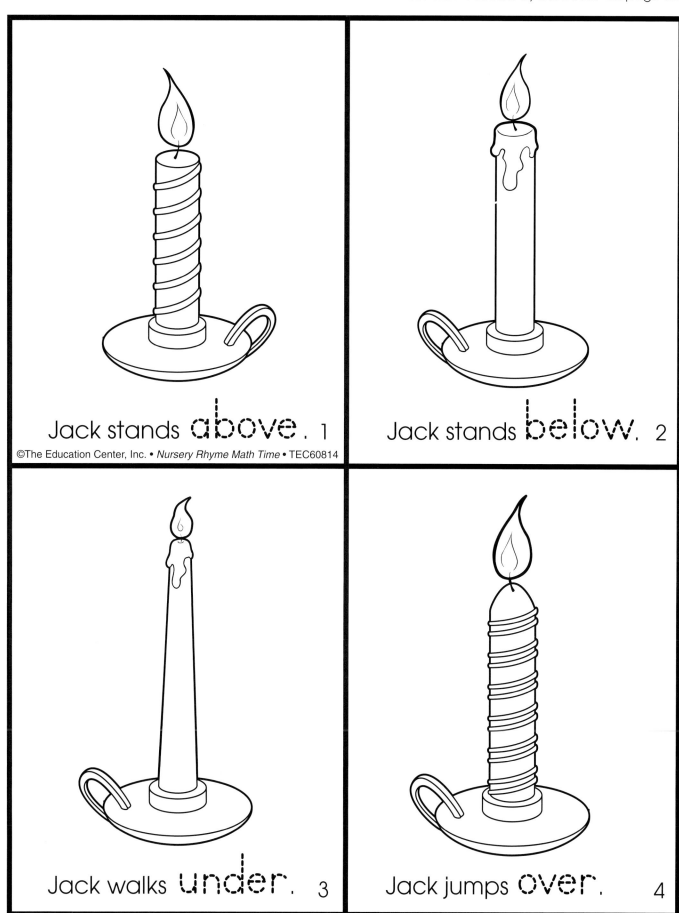

Jack stands **above**. 1

©The Education Center, Inc. • *Nursery Rhyme Math Time* • TEC60814

Jack stands **below**. 2

Jack walks **under**. 3

Jack jumps **over**. 4

This Little Piggy

Your little ones will be tickled pink with these little piggy activities!

This little piggy went to market;
This little piggy stayed home.
This little piggy had roast beef;
This little piggy had none.
This little piggy cried, "Wee, wee, wee!"
All the way home.

Pink Piggies
Number and Operations

• understanding one-to-one correspondence

Youngsters will enjoy putting each piggy in its place with this fun center activity. In advance, cut apart a copy of page 38. Color each card and then glue it onto a separate paper cup. Also gather five large pink pom-poms (piggies). Discuss the pictures on each prepared cup with your group and then lead them in counting the piggies. Ask students to recite the rhyme as you demonstrate placing one piggy in each corresponding cup. Then place the cups and piggies at a center and invite pairs of students to ham it up as they repeat the activity!

Piggy's Place
Geometry

• using positional words

This little piggy puppet reinforces youngsters' spatial skills and language skills. Give each child a copy of the puppet pattern on page 39 and a craft stick. Have each youngster color and cut out his piggy; then help him glue it onto a craft stick to make a puppet. Later, invite students to bring their puppets to circle time. Recite the rhyme with your group. Then ask youngsters to hold their puppets in front of their bodies and repeat, "This little piggy is in front of me." Continue the process with several different positional words. Then ask individual students to repeat the activity as the group watches and listens.

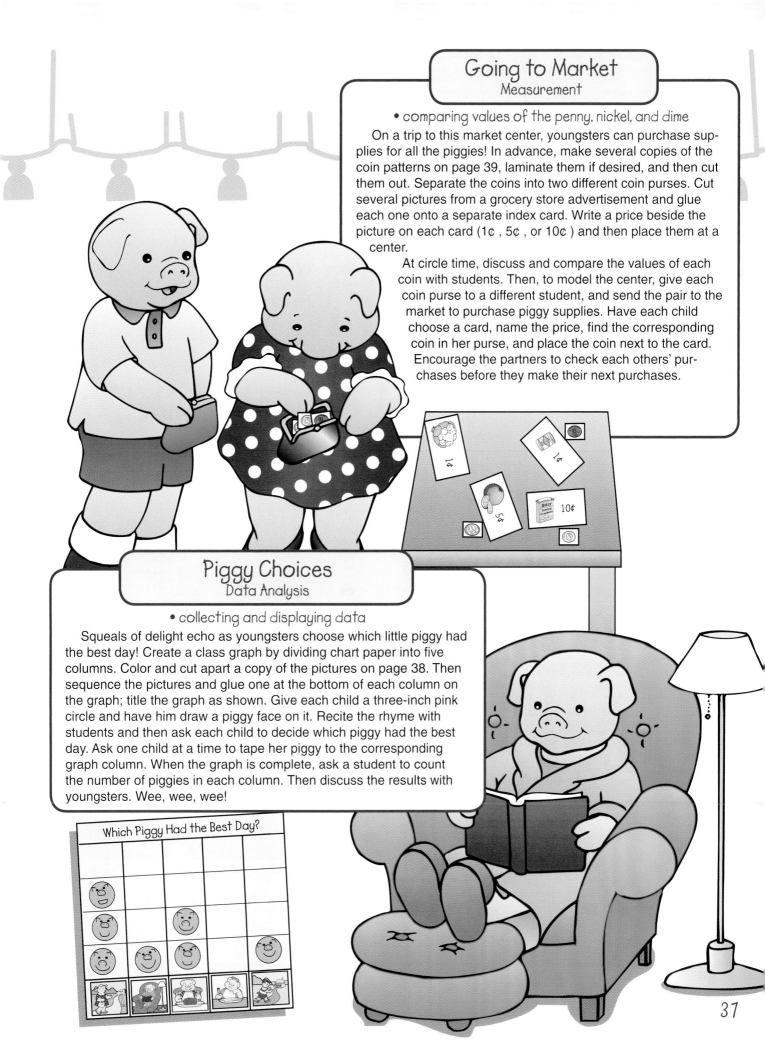

Going to Market
Measurement

• comparing values of the penny, nickel, and dime

On a trip to this market center, youngsters can purchase supplies for all the piggies! In advance, make several copies of the coin patterns on page 39, laminate them if desired, and then cut them out. Separate the coins into two different coin purses. Cut several pictures from a grocery store advertisement and glue each one onto a separate index card. Write a price beside the picture on each card (1¢ , 5¢ , or 10¢) and then place them at a center.

At circle time, discuss and compare the values of each coin with students. Then, to model the center, give each coin purse to a different student, and send the pair to the market to purchase piggy supplies. Have each child choose a card, name the price, find the corresponding coin in her purse, and place the coin next to the card. Encourage the partners to check each others' purchases before they make their next purchases.

Piggy Choices
Data Analysis

• collecting and displaying data

Squeals of delight echo as youngsters choose which little piggy had the best day! Create a class graph by dividing chart paper into five columns. Color and cut apart a copy of the pictures on page 38. Then sequence the pictures and glue one at the bottom of each column on the graph; title the graph as shown. Give each child a three-inch pink circle and have him draw a piggy face on it. Recite the rhyme with students and then ask each child to decide which piggy had the best day. Ask one child at a time to tape her piggy to the corresponding graph column. When the graph is complete, ask a student to count the number of piggies in each column. Then discuss the results with youngsters. Wee, wee, wee!

Picture Cards

Use with "Pink Piggies" on page 36 and "Piggy Choices" on page 37.

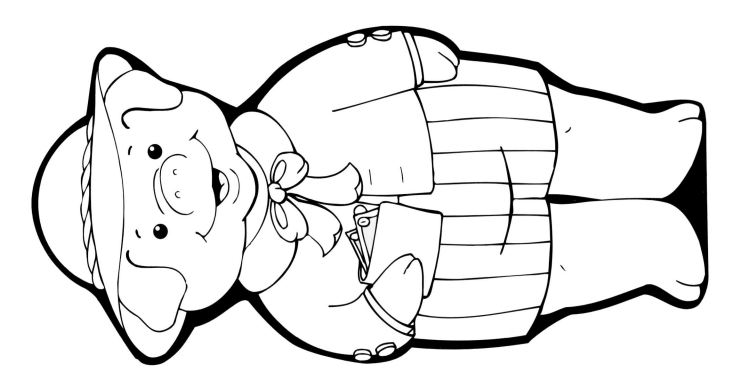

Coin Patterns
Use with "Going to Market" on page 37.

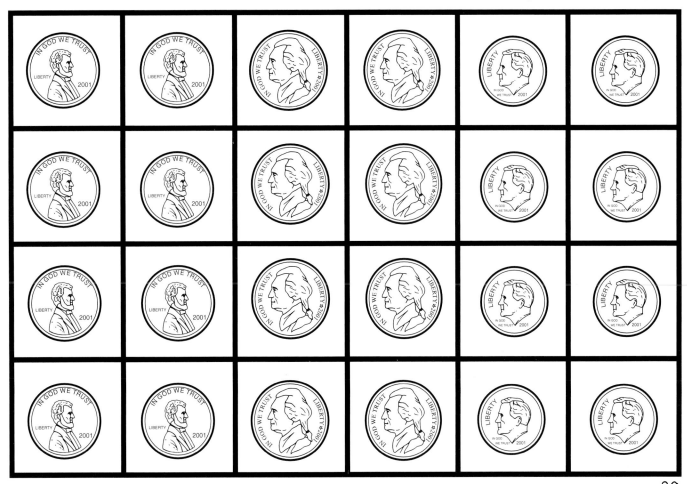

Jack and Jill

This eventful quest for a pail of water is filled to the brim
with playful math opportunities!

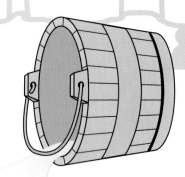

Jack and Jill
went up the
hill...

Jack and Jill went up the hill
To fetch a pail of water.
Jack fell down and broke his crown,
And Jill came tumbling after.

Up and Down
Geometry

• using positional words

Little ones gain greater understanding of the words *up* and
down when they use puppets to represent Jack and Jill at this
center! Place a stack of books on the floor in a center. Then lean
a board against the books to resemble a hill. Color a copy of
the patterns on page 42. Cut out the patterns and then laminate
them for durability. Tape the pail cutout to the top of the hill. Then
tape a craft stick to the back of each remaining cutout. Place
the resulting Jack and Jill stick puppets in the center. When your
class is comfortable reciting the rhyme without help, invite youngsters to the center two at a time. Each child takes a puppet. As
the students recite the rhyme, they use the puppets to show Jack
and Jill walking *up* the hill to the pail of water and then tumbling
down the hill. This center is sure to be a popular destination!

First Aid for Jack!
Geometry

• using positional words

With positional words and a few bandages, your youngsters will
have Jack patched up and as good as new! Make bandage manip-
ulatives by sticking each of 15 regular-size adhesive bandages
to a different same-size piece of tagboard. Make three copies of
page 43. Color and cut out the patterns. Then mount each cutout
on a 9" x 12" sheet of colored construction paper. Laminate the
resulting workmat for durability.

Next, gather a group of up to three children. Give each child a
workmat and provide access to the prepared bandages. Explain
that a few bandages will make Jack feel better after his fall. Give
the students an oral direction telling them where to place a bandage using one of the following positional words: *between, below,
above, on,* and *beside* (see suggestions provided). Then have
each child place a bandage in the location given. Continue until
each child has placed five bandages on his workmat and all the
positional words have been used.

Place a bandage *beside* Jack's nose.
Place a bandage *between* Jack's eyes.
Place a bandage *below* Jack's mouth.
Place a bandage *above* Jack's ear.
Place a bandage *on* Jack's cheek.

Fill It Up!
Measurement

• exploring tools for measuring capacity

Jack and Jill never did fill up their pail, but your youngsters can when they explore measurement tools with blue tinted rice instead of water! To tint rice blue, combine the following in a large resealable plastic bag: a one pound bag of white rice, 1½ tablespoons of rubbing alcohol, and several drops of blue food coloring. Mix the ingredients together by carefully shaking and manipulating the bag. Then spread the rice onto a large piece of aluminum foil for 24 hours or until dry. Prepare enough rice to fill a small plastic tub. Then place the filled tub at a center along with several measuring cups and spoons and a small pail. Before children visit the center, introduce the measuring tools. Then invite children to visit the center one at a time to explore the tools by measuring rice into the pail. This idea really measures up!

This one holds more!

Which Is Better?
Measurement

• comparing capacity

Which of these two containers would your youngsters give to Jack and Jill to take up the hill? The one that holds more water! Gather students in your large-group area and present two containers of different sizes. Explain that Jack and Jill can't find a pail to take up the hill and the two containers are all they have. Then explain that Jack and Jill want to take the container that holds more water. Invite students to guess which container holds more. Then use a plastic cup to fill each one with water as the children count the cupfuls. Compare the total cups of water needed to fill each container and then have the children determine whether their prediction was correct. If desired, place the containers and plastic cup at a water table for independent exploration.

One, Two, Buckle My Shoe
One, two, this action-packed unit is fun for youngsters to do!

> One, two, buckle my shoe.
> Three, four, knock at the door.
> Five, six, pick up sticks.
> Seven, eight, lay them straight.
> Nine, ten, a big fat hen.

Buckles or Not?
Algebra

• sorting by type

Buckle up for a fun comparison activity as youngsters take a closer look at their shoes. Gather youngsters on the carpet to recite the rhyme. Then discuss the meaning of "buckle my shoe." Ask youngsters to look at their shoes and decide whether they have buckles. Then have each child remove one shoe and place it in the middle of the circle. Help youngsters sort each type of shoe (buckle, Velcro fastener, tie, slip-on) into separate groups. Count out loud the shoes in each group and discuss the results with students. Invite a group of youngsters, according to shoe type, to stand in a row facing the class. Ask a volunteer to pair the correct shoe with each child in the group. Repeat the process until all the shoes have been paired. One, two, match my shoe!

Rhymin' Action
Number and Operations

• recognizing and naming written numerals

Pint-size performances of the traditional rhyme give youngsters practice with numeral recognition. To prepare, write the numerals 1–10 on separate index cards. Then invite ten students to stand in a row in front of the class. Tape one card onto the shirt of each child. Recite the rhyme out loud with the class and have each child step forward as his number is named. Repeat the rhyme slowly and have each child act out the verse that corresponds with his number (for example, one and two pretend to buckle their shoes).

To reinforce numeral recognition, help each child make a rhyme booklet from a copy of page 46. Have her color and cut out the booklet pages and then match and glue each number in the correct space provided. Next, sequence the pages and staple the booklet together along the left side.

Pick Up Sticks!
Number and Operations

• adding and subtracting with concrete objects

Pick up sticks or lay them straight to introduce youngsters to addition and subtraction. Gather a small group of children and have each child lay ten craft sticks on a table in front of her. Recite the rhyme and ask each child to manipulate her sticks according to the corresponding verses. Ask each youngster to count her sticks. Then give her directions to pick up sticks or lay them straight to illustrate subtraction and addition sentences. For example, you might say, "Lay ten sticks straight. Now pick up four sticks." After each child has followed your direction, ask her to count the remaining sticks. Then give another direction, such as "You have six sticks. Now lay down two sticks." Repeat the process several times. If desired, have each child create a number sentence by arranging and gluing her sticks on a piece of paper and then writing the corresponding numbers as shown.

Five Orderly Hens
Number and Operations

• sequencing ordinal numbers

Count on cute hens to help reinforce youngsters' ordinal counting skills. Gather your group and ask five hen volunteers to stand in a row facing the class. Lead students in ordinal counting of the hens (first, second, third, etc). As the class observes, call on each hen to do a task, such as "Third hen, flap your wings." Encourage the class to help each hen determine which ordinal number he represents. Repeat the activity with five different hens until each child has had a turn.

For additional practice, have each youngster complete a copy of page 47. Ask youngsters to listen and follow your oral directions, similar to those listed below.

1. Color the second hen red.
2. Draw a yellow sun over the fifth hen.
3. Draw a purple egg between the third and fourth hens.
4. Draw a hat on the first hen.
5. Draw a green apron on the third hen.

45

Booklet Cover and Pages

Use with "Rhymin' Action" on page 44.

1	2	3	4	5	6	7	8	9	10

One, Two

Name

©The Mailbox®

Pick up sticks.

Buckle my shoe.

Lay them straight.

Knock at the door.

A big fat hen.

Name _____

Five Fluffy Hens

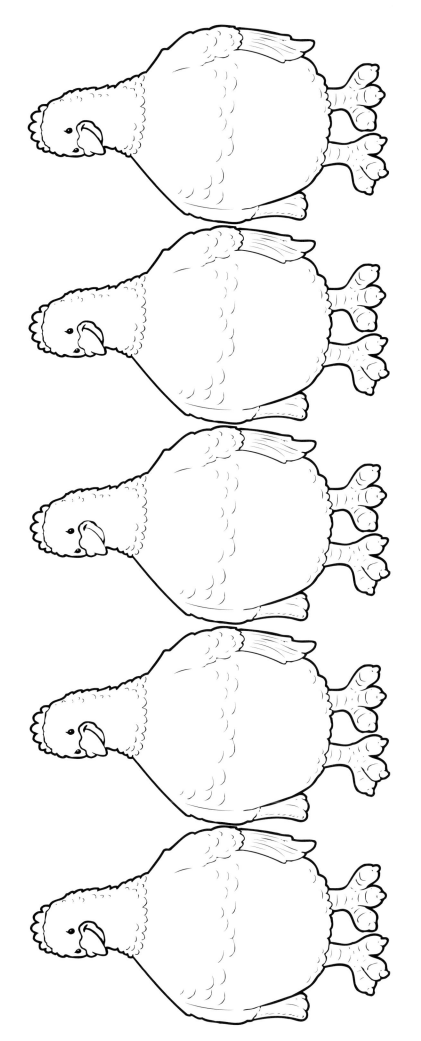

Note to the teacher: Use with "Five Orderly Hens" on page 45.

147

Old Mother Hubbard

A kindly lady and her faithful pooch are your little ones' guides through this unit stocked with learning opportunities!

Old Mother Hubbard
Went to the cupboard
To give her poor dog a bone;
But when she got there,
The cupboard was bare,
And so the poor dog had none.

From Full to Empty
Number and Operations

• understanding the concept of zero

Little ones peek into Mother Hubbard's cupboard to help them understand the concept of zero! Invite a small group of students to a table. Give each student crayons and a copy of page 50. Have her color the page and then write her name at the top. Also give each child a set of the bone cards on page 51 and a set of index cards labeled with numerals from 0 to 5. (Bone cards and index cards can be reused for each new group of students.) Each child places a bone card on each shelf on the cupboard, counts the number of bones, and then places the matching numeral card beside the cupboard. Next, she removes one bone at a time and places each appropriate numeral card on top of the previous one until she reaches 0. Finally, invite each youngster to practice writing the numeral 0 on each of the cupboard's shelves. This cupboard really is bare!

A Grateful Pooch!
Number and Operations

• subtracting with concrete objects

Cereal is the treat of choice for the little dogs in this subtraction activity! Give each child a copy of the dog pattern on page 51 and a small paper plate with ten pieces of cereal. Have her color and cut out the pattern. Recite the adjusted nursery rhyme provided. Each youngster places one piece of cereal on the dog when indicated. Then she counts the pieces remaining on her plate. When students decide how many are left, have them place all the cereal back on their plates. Recite the rhyme several times, substituting a different number under ten each time. When finished, invite little ones to eat their cereal. Tasty treats!

Old Mother Hubbard
Went to the cupboard
To get her poor dog a treat;
She gave [one] to the pooch,
Who gave her a smooch!
How many were left to eat?

A Book of Bones
Number and Operations

• using strategies to solve number problems

No bones about it, this class book filled with student-made addition pictures is bound to be a favorite in your classroom reading area! Cut bone shapes from house-hold sponges. Then hot-glue an empty film canister to the back of each one to create a handle. Place the prepared sponges and a shallow container of white paint at a table. Label a blue 12" x 18" sheet of construction paper with an addition problem for each child.

Next, invite a small group of students to the table. Give each child a prepared sheet of paper. Then explain that making a picture is one way to find the answer to an addition problem. Each child identifies the first numeral in the problem and then uses a prepared sponge to stamp a matching number of bone prints on the paper. He repeats the process with the second numeral. Then he counts all the bones and writes the answer to the prob-lem. When the paint is dry, bind the pages together in a book titled "Mother Hubbard's Addition Book."

Cans for the Cupboard
Number and Operations

• adding with concrete objects

After youngsters use the props for this addition center, they can be donated to help fill up empty cupboards just like Mother Hubbard's! Several days before the activity, send a note home requesting canned food donations. Next, label a sentence strip with a blank addition sen-tence, showing empty boxes for the numbers. Laminate the sentence strip. Then place the following items at a table in a center: the prepared strip, a dry-erase marker, a cloth (for erasing), two small boxes, and ten cans of the donated food.

A youngster visiting the center places a desired number of cans in a box. She writes the corresponding numeral in the first box on the sentence strip. Then she repeats the process with the remaining box and cans. She counts the cans in both boxes and writes the answer on the strip. The youngster erases the strip and repeats the activity. After each child has had a chance to visit the center, donate the cans of food to a local shelter.

49

How Many Bones?

Note to the teacher: Use with "From Full to Empty" on page 48.

Bone Cards
Use with "From Full to Empty" on page 48.

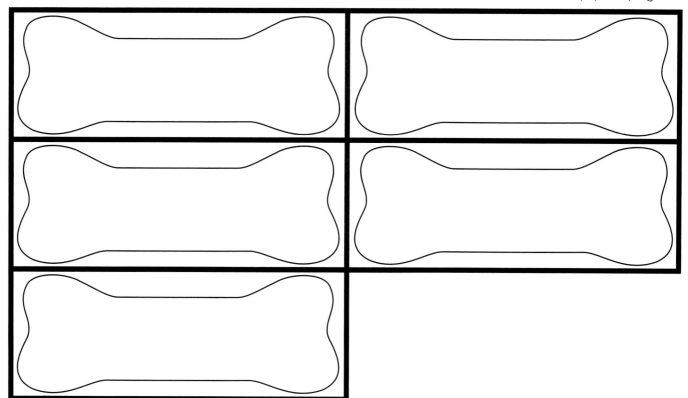

Dog Pattern
Use with "A Grateful Pooch!" on page 48.

Hickory, Dickory, Dock

This timely collection of math ideas keeps youngsters running back for more!

Hickory, dickory, dock,
The mouse ran up the clock;
The clock struck one,
And down he run,
Hickory, dickory, dock.

Shapely Clocks
Geometry

• identifying shapes

Little ones craft these creative clocks from four basic shapes! Use the guidelines provided to cut colorful construction paper into the following shapes (a class supply of each): rectangle, square, circle, and triangle. Sort the shapes into separate containers. Also make a class supply of the mouse pattern on page 54. Then place the prepared items at a table along with crayons and glue. Invite a small group of students to the table. Have each child choose and identify a shape from each container. Then help her glue the shapes together to make a clock like the one shown. Assist each student, if necessary, in adding numerals and hands to the clock face. Finally, have her color and cut out a mouse pattern and glue it to the clock. Ticktock!

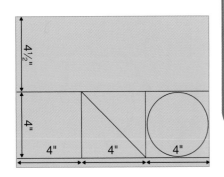

Clock Cover-Up!
Number and Operations

• recognizing numerals

Why should only one mouse run up the clock when there's room for 12 in this numeral identification activity? Make a brown construction paper copy of the mouse cards on page 54 for each child. Then cut apart the cards and place each set of 12 into a resealable plastic bag. Also make a copy of page 55. Write numerals on the clock; then make a copy for each child. Next, give each student a clock and a bag of cards. Call out a number from one to 12. Have him find the corresponding numeral on his clock and then cover it with a mouse card. Continue until each numeral has been covered with a card. Then have each youngster run all the mice down the clock and back into the bag!

Three.

Time to Run!
Measurement

• telling time to the hour

What time is it? It's time for a small-group game that combines movement with telling time on the hour! Make a set of flash cards showing digital times on the hour. Display a play clock at your children's eye level. Then gather a small group of students. Show one of the cards and have the children identify the time. Then recite the rhyme, replacing "one" with the time shown on the flash card. During the recitation, invite a youngster to pretend to be a mouse as he runs up to the play clock, moves the hands to the time shown on the card, and runs back to his seat. Choose a different student and time for each new run. Fun!

Where Are the Numerals?
Number and Operations

• writing numerals to 12

Hickory, dickory, dock—there aren't any numerals on this clock! Little ones fill in the missing numerals at this playful center. Make a copy of the mouse cards on page 54. Label the back of each card with a different number of dots from one to 12. Then laminate the cards and place them in a paper lunch bag. Also make a copy of page 55 for each pair of students. Place the prepared items at a table in a center. A pair of students visits the center and the students take turns removing a card from the bag, counting the dots, and then writing the corresponding numeral in the appropriate location on the clock. (If desired, provide a play clock or completed clock pattern for reference.) When all twelve numerals are written on the clock, the youngsters place the cards back in the bag for the next pair of students. This activity is time well spent!

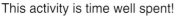

Mouse Pattern
Use with "Shapely Clocks" on page 52.

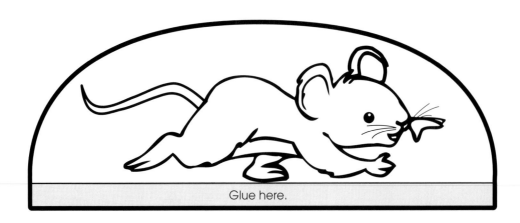

Glue here.

Mouse Cards
Use with "Clock Cover-Up!" on page 52 and "Where Are the Numerals?" on page 53.

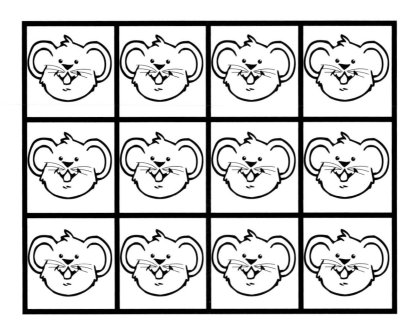

54

Use with "Clock Cover-Up!" on page 52 and "Where Are the Numerals?" on page 53.

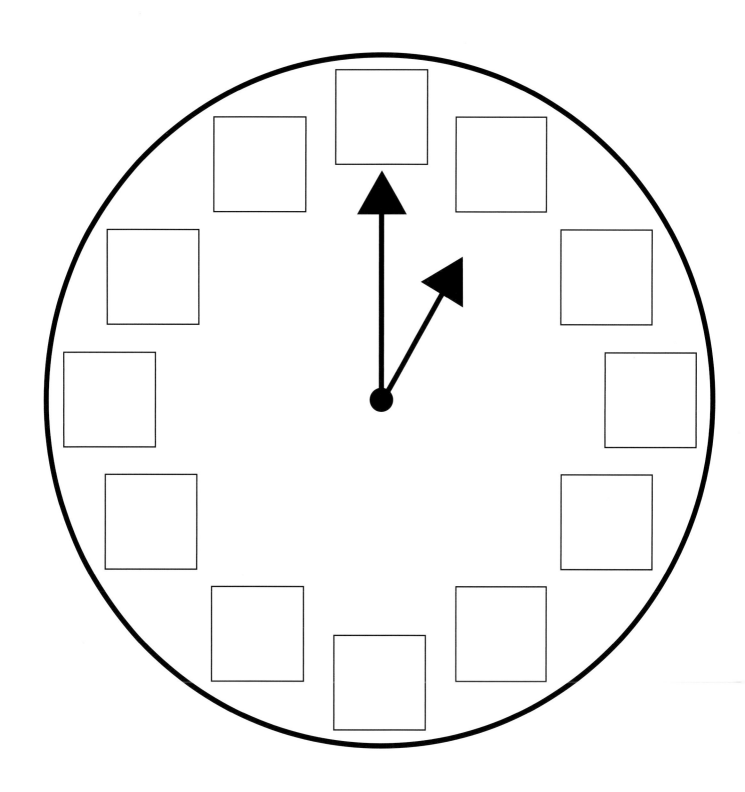

Sing a Song of Sixpence

Dish up a king-size portion of math practice with a cast of colorful characters and 24 feathered friends!

...23, 24.

> Sing a song of sixpence,
> A pocket full of rye;
> Four-and-twenty blackbirds
> Baked in a pie.
> When the pie was opened,
> The birds began to sing;
> Wasn't that a dainty dish
> To set before the king?
>
> The king was in his countinghouse,
> Counting out his money;
> The queen was in the parlor,
> Eating bread and honey.
> The maid was in the garden,
> Hanging out the clothes,
> When down flew a blackbird
> And pecked off her nose.

10¢   5¢   1¢

A Recipe for a Pie
Number and Operations

• counting to 24

Although this pie won't get many requests for dessert, it will certainly be a popular attraction at this counting center! To set up the center, cut twenty-four 2½-inch circles of black tagboard. Fold the circles in half, and decorate each one with a white crayon to resemble a blackbird as shown. Obtain an aluminum pie tin and cut a circle of brown construction paper to fit inside the tin (bottom crust) and a circle to sit on top of the tin (top crust). Add any desired decorations to the top crust. Place at a center the prepared cutouts, the pie tin, and a laminated copy of the blackbird pie recipe card on page 58. A youngster visits the center and follows the recipe, taking care to count out 24 blackbirds for the pie filling. That's a dessert fit for a king!

Money Bags
Measurement

• recognizing coin value (penny, nickel, dime)

Little ones sort coins by value in a center fit for a king! Make two copies of the coin cards and three yellow construction paper copies of the money bag pattern on page 59. Label the bags "1¢," "5¢," and "10¢" and color the coins appropriately. Then cut out the cards and patterns and laminate them for durability. Place the prepared items at a center along with a construction paper crown. A visiting youngster dons the crown. He chooses a coin cutout, identifies its value, and places it on the appropriate bag. He continues until each coin is placed on a bag. Then he removes the coins from the bags and leaves the crown, coins, and bags for the next visiting student. This center is a royal treasure!

Bread and Honey
Number and Operations

• adding to five with concrete objects

This honey of an idea sets youngsters up for sweet addition success! To prepare this small-group activity, cut out 20 squares of brown construction paper (bread slices). Drizzle each square with some yellow paint (honey) if desired. Then set the squares aside to dry. Also prepare four large circular workmats from white construction paper (plates). Place the prepared items at a table. Then invite a group of up to four students to join you. Give each student a plate and access to the bread slices. Next, instruct her to follow your oral directions to find the sums for addition problems similar to the example provided. Consider serving a snack of bread and honey as a tasty finale to this activity!

The queen put three slices of bread on her plate.
The queen added two more slices.
How many slices of bread are on the plate?

Counting Clothing
Number and Operations

• comparing two sets

Present this laundry-themed comparison activity to your little ones and they're sure to hang around! Prior to the day of the activity, give each child a copy of the shirt pattern (page 58) to decorate. Then cut out the shirts and laminate them for durability.

Set up this small-group activity by placing the shirts at a table along with two sentence strips (clotheslines), a large foam die, and a supply of clothespins. Invite a pair of students to the table. A student rolls the die and then clips that number of shirts to a clothesline. The other child repeats the process, clipping shirts to the second clothesline. The students compare strips and identify who has more shirts, who has less, or whether they both have the same number. Laundry has never been so much fun!

Recipe Card

Use with "A Recipe for a Pie" on page 56.

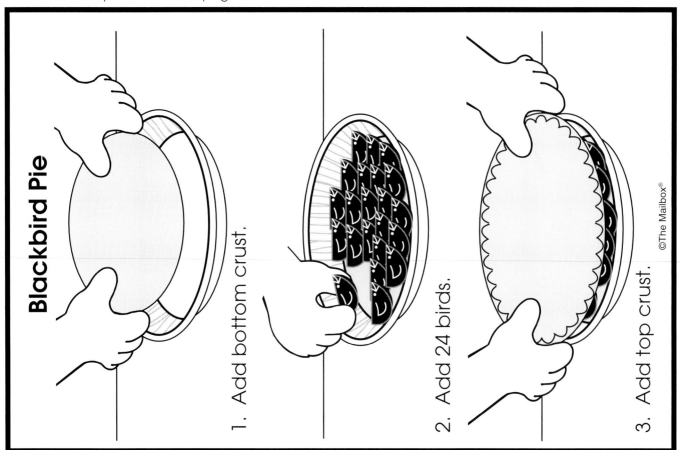

Blackbird Pie

1. Add bottom crust.

2. Add 24 birds.

3. Add top crust.

©The Mailbox®

Shirt Pattern

Use with "Counting Clothing" on page 57.

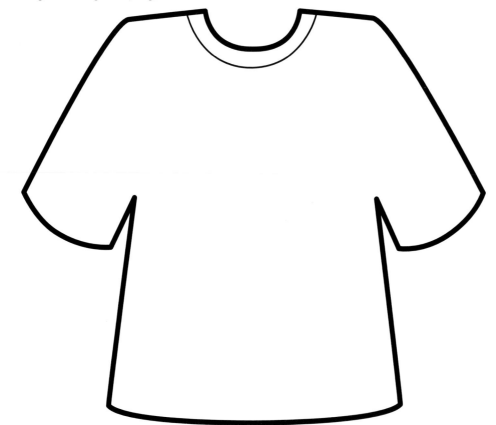

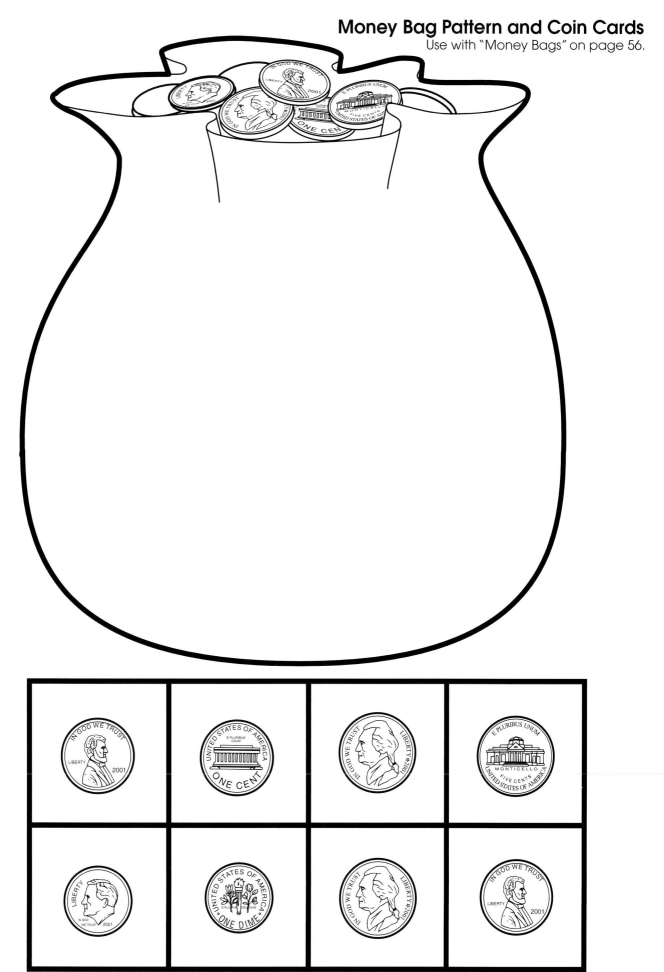

A Tisket, a Tasket
Fill your basket with these fun activities!

A tisket, a tasket,
A green and yellow basket.
I wrote a letter to my love,
But on the way I dropped it.
I dropped it, I dropped it,
And on the way I dropped it.
A little boy picked it up
And put it in his pocket.

Lost-and-Found Letters
Number and Operations

• adding and subtracting with concrete objects

Put that green and yellow basket to good use in this circle-time activity! To prepare, place ten sealed envelopes (or copies of the letter patterns on page 62) and a basket in your circle area. With student help, say the nursery rhyme aloud and then place one letter in the basket. Next, ask a volunteer to add another letter to the basket and count how many in all. Continue adding letters until all ten are in the basket. Invite a student to hold the basket and skip around the circle while the class chants the rhyme. At the appropriate moment, have the student drop one letter. Say the matching number sentence and encourage youngsters to figure out how many are left in the basket. Continue subtracting letters in this manner until all are gone.

A Pocketful of Letters
Algebra

• sorting and classifying objects

What if the little boy who found the lost letter found several? He would need to sort them in order to return the correct letter! In advance, gather a supply of colored envelopes in a variety of sizes. (Or copy the patterns on page 62 to make a supply of letters in various sizes, shapes, and colors.) Place the envelopes and a child's carpenter apron in a center. To use the center, a student pretends to have lost her letter. She looks at the envelopes and chooses a single attribute to describe her letter, such as a color. Her partner dons the apron and then picks up the envelopes that do not share the attribute and puts them into the apron pocket. She checks the remaining envelopes and chooses a different attribute to describe her letter, such as a shape. He sorts the envelopes and puts the ones that do not match into his pocket. She checks the remaining envelope(s) again and selects the one that is "hers." Invite the pair to switch roles and sort the envelopes again in this same manner. Encourage each child to take several turns in each role.

My letter is not pink.

These are pink.

60

Here is my basket.
I think it will hold **20**
I counted. It holds **11**

How Large Is Your Basket?
Measurement

• estimating capacity

A tisket, a tasket, how much fills your basket? Explore concepts of capacity with this cool comparision activity. In advance, stock a center with different sizes and colors of baskets, a quantity of large teddy bear counters, and a class supply of the recording sheet on page 63. To use the center, a child draws one basket on her recording sheet where indicated and estimates how many counters will fill it to capacity. Next, she fills the basket with counters and compares her estimate with the actual amount. Then she uses that information to estimate the capacity of another basket. She continues in this manner until each basket's capacity has been measured. Hey, the green basket holds more than the yellow basket!

Letter Love
Data Analysis

• collecting and displaying data

Who is the special love referred to in the rhyme? Could it be a mother or father? A grandparent? Find out with this graphing activity! Help each child write (or dictate as you write) a letter to a loved one and seal it in an addressed envelope. Next, display the results on a large floor graph. Program the columns similar to those shown; then invite each child who wrote a letter to her mother to place it on a corresponding cell. Continue with each family category, in turn, until all the letters are graphed. Compare and discuss the results with students. Then have each child take home her letter to be mailed or given to the lucky loved one.

| mother | father | grandmother | grandfather |

Letter Patterns

Use with "Lost-and-Found Letters" and "A Pocketful of Letters" on page 60.

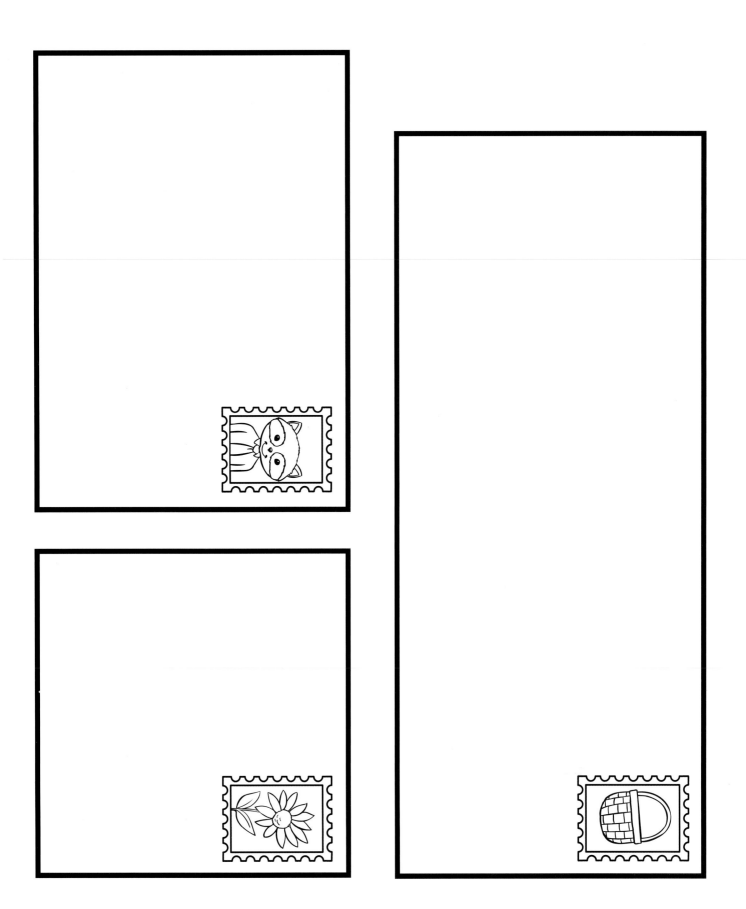

A Full Basket

Here is my basket.

I think it will hold _____.

I counted. It holds _____.

Managing Editor: Cindy K. Daoust

Editorial Team: Becky S. Andrews, Kimberley Bruck, Karen P. Shelton, Diane Badden, Thad H. McLaurin, Susan Walker, Kimberly A. Brugger, Leanne Stratton, Allison E. Ward, Karen A. Brudnak, Sarah Hamblet, Hope Rodgers, Dorothy C. McKinney

Production Team: Lisa K. Pitts, Ivy L. Koonce (COVER ARTIST), Pam Crane, Clevell Harris, Rebecca Saunders, Jennifer Tipton Bennett, Chris Curry, Theresa Lewis Goode, Ivy L. Koonce, Clint Moore, Greg D. Rieves, Barry Slate, Donna K. Teal, Tazmen Carlisle, Amy Kirtley-Hill, Kristy Parton, Debbie Shoffner, Cathy Edwards Simrell, Lynette Dickerson, Mark Rainey